SUPER

Animal Origami Crafts

By Jill Smolinski

Illustrated by Charlene Olexiewicz

LOWELL HOUSE JUVENILE

LOS ANGELES

CONTEMPORARY BOOKS

CHICAGO

To Alex and Erin Smolinski, who love all kinds of animals—even paper ones!

NOTE: The numbered pinwheel in the upper right-hand corner of each craft indicates the level of difficulty, 1 being the easiest, 3 being the hardest.

Publisher: Jack Artenstein
Director of Publishing Services: Rena Copperman
Editorial Director, Juvenile: Brenda Pope-Ostrow
Director of Juvenile Development: Amy Downing
Typesetter: Treesha Runnells
Cover Crafts Artist: Charlene Olexiewicz
Cover Photograph: Ann Bogart

Lowell House books can be purchased at special discounts when ordered in bulk for premiums and special sales. Contact Department TC at the following address:

Lowell House Juvenile
2020 Avenue of the Stars, Suite 300
Los Angeles, CA 90067

Library of Congress Catalog Card Number: 97-76093

ISBN: 1-56565-928-7

Printed in the United States of America

10 9 8 7 6 5 4 3 2 1

Contents

Before You Begin 4

Basic Folds 4

Basic Forms 5

1. Paper-Doodle-Do! 11
2. Pecking Crow 12
3. Eeek! A Mouse! 13
4. Fishy Friend 14
5. Cute Cricket 15
6. From Square to Hare 16
7. Ready to Roar 17
8. Wild and Woolly 18
9. Super Simple Seagull 19
10. A Pest with Pizzazz 20
11. Raccoon Cap 22
12. Homing Pigeon 23
13. Thar She Blows! 24
14. Leapfrog 26
15. Barking Dog 27
16. One Slippery Snake 28
17. Dog or Cat House 30
18. Kangaroo's Pouch 31
19. The World's Fastest Turtle . . .32
20. Terrific Tiger 34
21. A Forest for Furry Friends . . .35
22. Lucky Ladybug 36
23. Happy Crab, Crabby Crab . . .38
24. Swan Lake 39
25. Goin' Batty 40

26. A Barn for Your Brood 42
27. Crazy Critter Mask 44
28. One-Ton Elephant 46
29. Gentle Giraffe 48
30. A Perfect Penguin 50
31. Flapping Bird 51
32. Snapping Alligator 52
33. A Family of Butterflies 54
34. Circus Seal 56
35. Nest, Sweet Nest 58
36. A Whale of a Goat 59
37. Handsome Hamster 60
38. Friendly Gorilla 62
39. Here, Piggy, Piggy! 64
40. Puff, Puff, Puffer Fish 66
41. Dinnertime! 68
42. A Horse, of Course 70
43. Crazy Like a Fox 72
44. Wise Old Owl 73
45. Paper Panda 74
46. Fluffy Bunny 76
47. Fabulous Flamingo 77
48. Snorting Bull 78
49. Tom Turkey 79
50. Origami Ark 80

Before You Begin

When does an alligator look like an elephant? Or a mouse like a monkey? When you're folding origami animals, they all look alike at one point—that is, before you begin! Each origami craft starts as a simple square of paper. With a few folds, you can whip up all kinds of animals—from creatures with wings to those with fins, and even a few with fangs!

In creating your origami crafts, any thin, square paper will do. Special origami paper is available at art supply and specialty stores, and wrapping paper also works well. For the best results, fold the paper neatly and carefully, especially at the corners. Work on a clean surface, and follow each step closely. In origami, the fun is in the folding as well as in the finished product, so take your time and skip the shortcuts.

Step-by-step instructions are included for each project. There are three basic folds you will use throughout this book:

Basic Folds

Valley Fold

Fold the paper toward you.

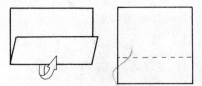

Mountain Fold

Fold the paper away from you.

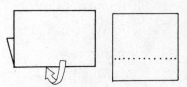

Squash Fold

This fold is used when two sides of a flap need to be squashed flat. To do this, poke your finger inside the flap and—you guessed it—squash it.

Origami crafts begin with one of many basic forms. Here you'll learn the forms that are the foundation for some of the origami projects in the book.

Basic Form 1

1. Begin with a square piece of paper in a flat diamond shape, color side facedown. Fold your paper in half, bringing the left point to meet the right point. Then unfold.

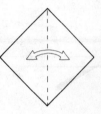

2. Fold the left and right points to the center crease so your paper looks like a kite.

Basic Form 2

1. Begin with a piece of origami paper in a flat diamond shape, color side facedown. Fold your paper in half, bringing the bottom point to meet the top.

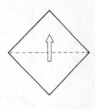

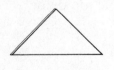

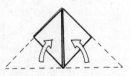

2. Now fold the far left and right points toward the center so the points meet at the top of your form.

Basic Form 3

1. Begin with a square piece of paper in a flat square shape, color side facedown. Fold your paper in half by bringing the top edge to meet the bottom edge, then fold it in half again by folding the left side to meet the right side. Reopen it into a square.

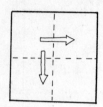

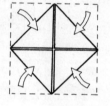

2. Next, fold each of the four corners to the center point, where the two creases made in Step 1 cross.

Basic Form 4

1. First, complete the instructions for Basic Form 1, then fold the top left and right sides (at the wide end of the kite) to the center line and make two sharp creases. Now fold the form in half, bringing the bottom point to meet the top point.

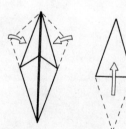

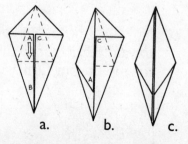

a.   b.   c.

2. Carefully open the form back to a kite. Then, while holding down point B with your fingertip, lift point A up and fold it down along the center line to point B. Crease form flat. Repeat the same fold with point C.

Basic Form 5

1. To make this form, begin with a square, color side facedown. Fold your paper in half from side to side, then fold it in half from top to bottom. Open it up to the original square and fold it diagonally both ways. Reopen it.

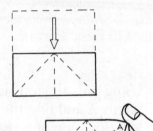

2. Once more, fold down the top edge to meet the bottom edge. Hold the right side of the form open at point A, then push point A down inside the form with a squash fold to meet point B. Crease the form flat.

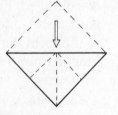

3. Repeat step 2 with the left side, and your form is ready.

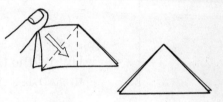

Basic Form 6

1. First, do step 1 in Basic Form 5.

2. Lay the origami square in front of you in a diamond shape, color side face-down. Fold the paper in half, bringing the top point to meet the bottom point.

3. Carefully hold the right side of the form open at point A, then squash-fold point A to the inside of the form to meet point B. Does it look like the illustration here?

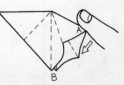

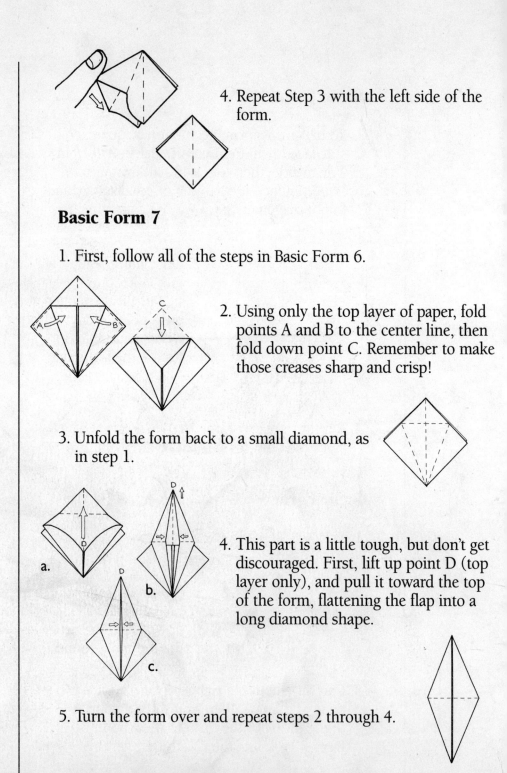

4. Repeat Step 3 with the left side of the form.

Basic Form 7

1. First, follow all of the steps in Basic Form 6.

2. Using only the top layer of paper, fold points A and B to the center line, then fold down point C. Remember to make those creases sharp and crisp!

3. Unfold the form back to a small diamond, as in step 1.

a.

b.

c.

4. This part is a little tough, but don't get discouraged. First, lift up point D (top layer only), and pull it toward the top of the form, flattening the flap into a long diamond shape.

5. Turn the form over and repeat steps 2 through 4.

Basic Form 8

1. Complete step 1 in Basic Form 5, then unfold your paper so it is lying flat. Fold the right and left sides so they meet the center line.

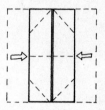

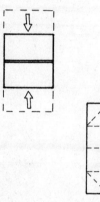

2. Now fold the bottom and top edges so they meet the center line. Make nice sharp creases, then unfold the paper. Your form should now look like the second illustration here.

3. Make two diagonal creases across the center four squares only. Do this by first folding point A to meet point B. Crease the paper sharply, then unfold it. Now repeat on the opposite side, bringing point C to meet point D, then unfold it. Your form should look like the last illustration here.

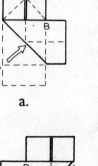

a.

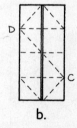

b.

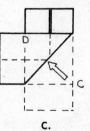

c.

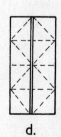

d.

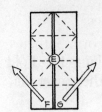

4. This next step is tricky, so look closely at the illustration for help. While holding down point E, lift up points F and G, pulling them apart and up toward the center line. Flatten the form. Repeat this step with points H and I.

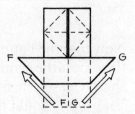

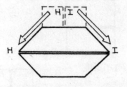

Paper-Doodle-Do!

Create a cute rooster that's really worth crowing about!

What You'll Need

• white origami paper • scissors • scraps of red and white paper
• glue • black and yellow markers

Directions

1. Begin with Basic Form 1, and lay it so the long pointed end faces right. Fold the form in half by bringing the top to the bottom.

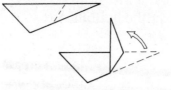

2. Make a diagonal crease about a third of the way in from the right point by folding and unfolding your form.

3. To make the tail, pick up the form and reopen it as shown. Hold the left side in your left hand, and push the right point back in a mountain fold, allowing the form to bend at the dotted line. Continue pushing back on the point until the form automatically recloses in half. Crease the form flat.

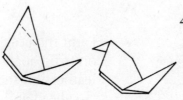

4. Make a beak by folding and unfolding the upper left point as shown. Open up the form slightly and squash-fold the point inside the head, forming the beak.

5. Cut a crown from the red paper, and glue it on top of your rooster's head. Cut out two wings from the white paper, and glue them onto the rooster's sides. Finally, draw on an eye with the black marker, and color in his beak with the yellow marker.

11

2 Pecking Crow

Here is origami in action! Make a hungry crow that pecks at the ground no matter how many times you try to set him straight.

What You'll Need

- black origami paper • paintbrush • orange paint
- two googly eyes • glue • three feathers

Directions

1. Start with Basic Form 1, then turn it on its side with the long point facing left. Fold the form in half by bringing the top to meet the bottom.

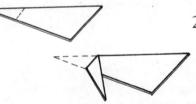

2. Make a crease by folding and unfolding your form on the dotted line as shown in the illustration.

3. Your crow can't peck without a beak! To give him one, squash-fold the left point down, tucking it between the two sides of the form.

4. Paint the beak orange, and glue on two googly eyes. Glue on feathers for the wings and a tail. Go ahead and try to stand the crow on his base. He'll automatically tip over to "peck" at the ground!

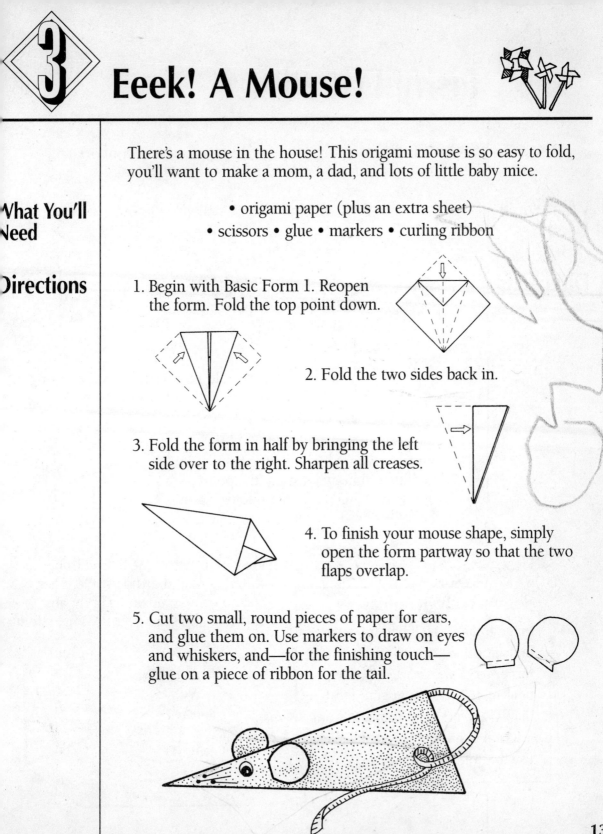

Eeek! A Mouse!

There's a mouse in the house! This origami mouse is so easy to fold, you'll want to make a mom, a dad, and lots of little baby mice.

What You'll Need

- origami paper (plus an extra sheet)
- scissors • glue • markers • curling ribbon

Directions

1. Begin with Basic Form 1. Reopen the form. Fold the top point down.

2. Fold the two sides back in.

3. Fold the form in half by bringing the left side over to the right. Sharpen all creases.

4. To finish your mouse shape, simply open the form partway so that the two flaps overlap.

5. Cut two small, round pieces of paper for ears, and glue them on. Use markers to draw on eyes and whiskers, and—for the finishing touch— glue on a piece of ribbon for the tail.

4 Fishy Friend

You'll find that sea creatures are a favorite subject of origami enthusiasts. You can make this little fish in minutes.

What You'll Need

• origami paper • markers • glue • glitter

Directions

1. Begin with Basic Form 1, then fold down the top point so it touches the wide horizontal line.

2. Now fold your form in half by bringing the left side to meet the right.

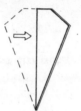

3. The pointed end is your fish's tail. You can make yours look like the fish's tail in the illustration by grasping the point and folding it, using a mountain fold. Flatten the fold well so the tail stays in place.

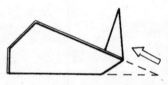

4. Give your fish some flair with big, round eyes and a wide smile. Then spread some glue on its body, and sprinkle glitter all over it. What shiny scales!

Truly Tropical

In the tropics, you'll find fish with brilliant colors and wild designs, like this peacock wrasse. Check out a book on tropical fish at your local library, and use watercolors to paint a school of origami fish so they look like the "reel" deal.

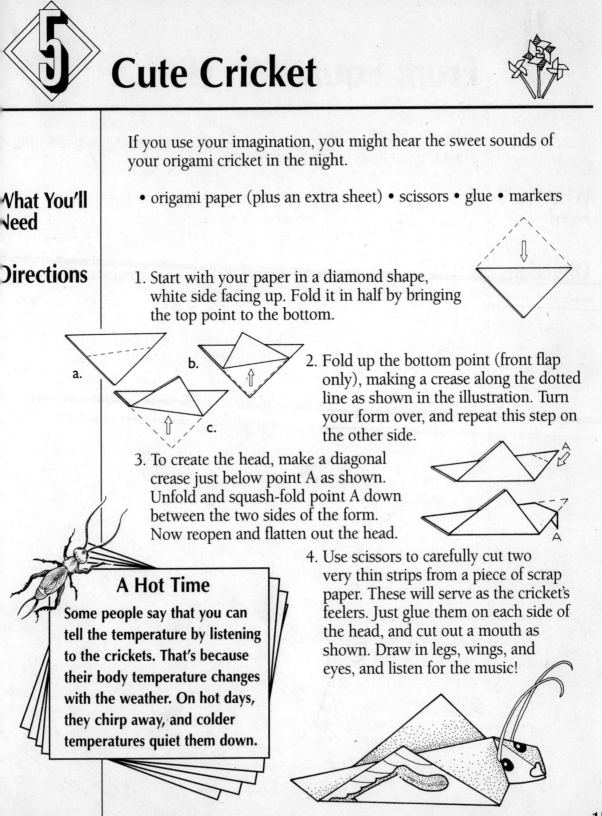

5 Cute Cricket

If you use your imagination, you might hear the sweet sounds of your origami cricket in the night.

What You'll Need

• origami paper (plus an extra sheet) • scissors • glue • markers

Directions

1. Start with your paper in a diamond shape, white side facing up. Fold it in half by bringing the top point to the bottom.

a.

b.

c.

2. Fold up the bottom point (front flap only), making a crease along the dotted line as shown in the illustration. Turn your form over, and repeat this step on the other side.

3. To create the head, make a diagonal crease just below point A as shown. Unfold and squash-fold point A down between the two sides of the form. Now reopen and flatten out the head.

4. Use scissors to carefully cut two very thin strips from a piece of scrap paper. These will serve as the cricket's feelers. Just glue them on each side of the head, and cut out a mouth as shown. Draw in legs, wings, and eyes, and listen for the music!

A Hot Time

Some people say that you can tell the temperature by listening to the crickets. That's because their body temperature changes with the weather. On hot days, they chirp away, and colder temperatures quiet them down.

15

6 From Square to Hare

You won't believe how a basic square-shaped form is just two simple folds away from becoming a cuddly bunny!

What You'll Need

• origami paper • scissors • glue • pink felt
• marker • cotton ball

Directions

1. Begin with Basic Form 5 (open flaps facing upward to the right as shown).

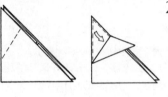

2. Use a valley fold to fold the top left corner over so it sticks out over the long edge. The crease should not begin at the bottom corner, but a little higher up. Turn the form over and repeat this step.

3. Set it down and you'll see that this rabbit can already stand on its own! Just glue felt triangles onto the ears, and use a marker to draw on eyes, back legs, and whiskers. To add a fuzzy tail, glue a cotton ball in between the two outer sides.

Ready to Roar

Fold a mighty lion finger puppet that's king of the jungle—and star of the show!

What You'll Need

- origami paper, 5 to 6 inches square (plus an extra sheet)
- clear tape • markers • scissors • glue • yarn

Directions

1. Lay the paper down, white side up. Fold Basic Form 1, then turn it so the wider end is toward you.

2. Turn the form over. Fold the left and right bottom edges to the center line.

3. Now fold the form in half by bringing the bottom point to meet the top using a valley fold. To make the lion's beard, fold down only the front flap so it just touches the bottom edge of your form.

4. Flip the form over and grasp the lower right and left corners, then curve them around so your form is in the shape of a tube. To secure it in place, slide the right bottom point between the two layers in the other side, and secure it with tape. Two of your fingers should fit inside the tube.

5. Fold the top point down as shown and secure it with a piece of tape. Turn the form over and use markers to draw your lion's face. Cut out two ears from the extra paper and glue them on the head. Glue on pieces of yarn around his crown as a mane.

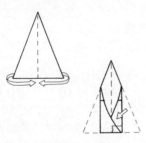

Wild and Woolly

Why not fashion a furry, woolly lamb friend for your lion puppet?

What You'll Need

• white origami paper, 8 inches square • markers • scissors • white pipe cleaners • pencil • tape • pink felt • glue

Directions

1. With a square piece of paper, fold the left side to the right, crease, then unfold. Fold the two sides toward the center line.

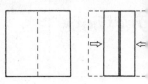

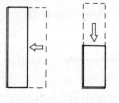

2. Fold the form in half by folding the right side over to meet the left side, then bring the top edge down to the bottom.

3. See how you've made two flaps of several layers each? Fold the front flap up halfway. Turn the form over and repeat this step on the other flap.

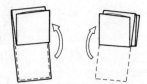

4. If you put your index finger inside the pocket of the top flap and your thumb in the bottom, you can see that your little lamb is ready to speak. Not baaaaaaad!

5. To make a cute lamb face, use markers to draw facial features on the top flap. Then use scissors to cut three pipe cleaners into 6-inch pieces and wind each piece around a pencil to make it curly. Tape the curls around the lamb's face. Open up the mouth and draw in teeth, then color the inside of the mouth black. Cut out a nose, two ears, and a tongue from pink felt and glue them on the lamb.

Super Simple Seagull

Turn your bedroom into a seaside paradise by creating a flock of seagulls, then attach a piece of thread or string to hang them.

What You'll Need

- white origami paper, at least 8 inches square
- yellow, orange, and black markers • scissors • thread • tape

Directions

1. Begin with a square piece of paper in a flat diamond shape. Fold it in half by bringing the bottom point to meet the top.

2. Fold the top point down so that it slightly overlaps the bottom edge.

3. Fold the form in half again so that the top edge meets the bottom straight edge. Fold the top to the bottom one more time.

 a.

b.

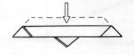

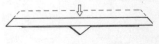

4. Bring the two wings together so they touch at the tips, then fold them out and down at a slight angle as shown. Allow the form to open up a little.

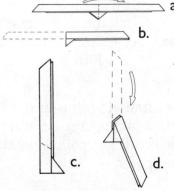 c. d.

5. Color the beak yellow, and add a tiny orange dot on the side to make the gull's "beauty mark." Put two black dots above the beak for eyes. Cut a 6-inch length of thread, and tape the two ends of the thread to each wing. Cut another length of thread to use as the hanger, attaching it to the center of the first thread. Hang your beautiful bird from the ceiling.

A Pest with Pizzazz

Use brightly colored paper to make a paper pest that could never bug anyone!

What You'll Need

• origami paper, 8 inches square • pipe cleaner • tape • glue • two googly eyes • paintbrush • puff paints

Directions

1. With your paper in a diamond shape, fold it in half by bringing the top point down to the bottom.

2. Fold the top edge down toward you a half-inch. Crease it sharply, then unfold.

3. Fold the bottom point (front flap only) up to about an inch below the straight edge.

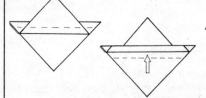

4. Roll this new crease up to the straight edge. See the band across the middle of your form?

5. Look closely at the illustration for this next step. Bring the bottom point up, creasing it at the base of the middle band. The point should extend above the other point.

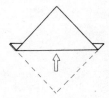

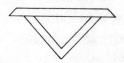

6. Turn the form over and lay it pointed side facing down.

7. Fold point A with a mountain fold behind the form so the tip slightly overlaps the far right edge. Repeat this step for point B. Your bug is ready to buzz!

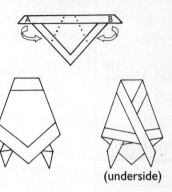

(underside)

8. Add antennae by folding a piece of pipe cleaner in half and taping it to the underside of the form. Glue on two googly eyes. Then use puff paints to add designs to the back to give your paper pest personality.

What's the Buzz?

Want a great card—fast? Glue one of your origami animals to the front of a stiff piece of paper that has been folded in half, and you have a 3-D card that's also a work of art. You can use the pest to decorate a get-well card that says, "I heard you got the 'BUG'!"

Raccoon Cap

If you can't find gray paper to make this classic raccoon cap, use a brown bag instead and decorate it to look like any animal you want!

What You'll Need

• gray paper, about 24 inches square • thick black marker • scissors • gray felt • glue

Directions

1. Begin with Basic Form 2, then turn the paper over so the two front flaps are on the bottom. Fold them up to make the raccoon's ears.

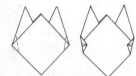

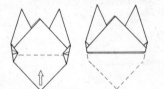

a.   b.   c.

2. Fold the bottom point up (front flap only) so it meets the point at the top. Turn your form over.

3. Use a valley fold to fold the left and right corners in as shown.

4. Now fold the form in half by bringing the bottom point up to meet the top.

5. To complete your cap, just fold down the top point and turn the form over.

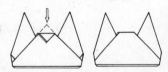

6. Use a black marker to draw a raccoon face on the front of the cap. You can copy the drawing here, or make up one of your own. Cut out a tail from the felt, draw black stripes on it, and glue it to the back of the cap.

Homing Pigeon

Toss this bird into the air and—just like a real homing pigeon—it flies back to you.

What You'll Need

• origami paper • colored pencils

Directions

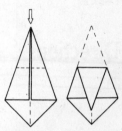

1. Begin with Basic Form 1, and turn it so that the narrow point is at the top. Fold the narrow point down just below the horizontal line.

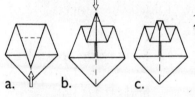

a.   b.   c.

2. Now fold that point up again so it sticks above the top of the form. Fold it back down again partway, and turn the form over.

3. Fold the left side diagonally toward the center so the top left point touches the center line. Repeat this step on the right side.

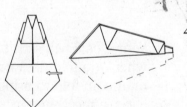

4. Turn the form over again. Valley-fold the form in half, bringing the right side to the left. The long, straight edge is the bottom of your bird.

5. Add the finishing touches by drawing on a beak, eyes, and feathers. Ready to send your homing pigeon soaring? Grasp it at the bottom and throw it overhand. Aim up, rather than straight ahead, and it will sail back to you.

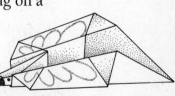

Thar She Blows!

Do you think you need a boat and binoculars to spot a whale? All you really need is a square piece of paper to have a whale of a time!

What You'll Need

• origami paper • marker • scissors
• curling ribbon (white or light blue) • tape

Directions

1. Begin with Basic Form 1, and turn the form so the narrow point faces right. Use a mountain fold to turn the left point back so it touches the baseline (that's the horizontal line formed when two folded sides meet).

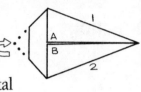

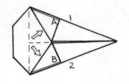

2. Now bring point A to meet side 1 and crease flat. Bring point B to meet side 2 and crease flat.

3. Using a valley fold, fold points C and D along the dotted lines as shown in the illustration.

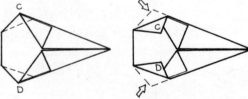

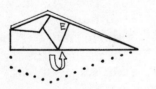

4. Your whale will start to take shape when you fold the form in half, using a mountain fold to bring the bottom side back to meet the top.

5. See the folded flap that runs diagonally through the center of the whale's body? To form a flipper, fold point E down so it touches the flap, about two-thirds of the way down. Then fold point F up almost to the top of the form. Repeat this step on the other side.

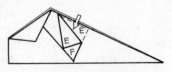

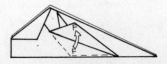

6. Give it a whale of a tail by folding the right point upward. Use a marker to draw in the eyes and a big smile! To make a spout, cut three lengths of curling ribbon. Slightly curl one end of each ribbon, and tape the three ribbons onto the top of the whale.

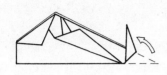

A Whale of a Game

Play a fun fishing game by folding ten whales, then numbering them 1 through 10. Attach a paper clip to each. Make a fishing pole by tying a stick to one end of a piece of string and a magnet to the other. Lay the whales where they can't be seen, such as behind a couch. Then take turns fishing with a friend, lowering the pole to try to catch whales with the magnet. Add up the score based on the number written on each whale. The player with the most points is the winner. Of course, because many whales are endangered, be sure to toss your catches back . . . and play again!

14 Leapfrog

Make two of these paper frogs, then challenge a friend to a good old-fashioned frog race.

What You'll Need

- green origami paper • glue • two googly eyes
- dark green or brown marker

Directions

1. Begin with Basic Form 3, then set it in front of you in a diamond shape. Fold the left and right points inward to meet at the center line.

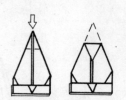

2. Fold the bottom point up to the center of the form.

3. Now fold the left and right corners to the center. If your form looks like a house with a pointed roof, you're "hopping" right along!

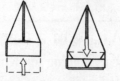

4. Bring the bottom edge up so it just touches the bottom of the "roof," then fold it halfway back down.

5. Fold the top point about a third of the way down the form, then flip the form over. Glue on two googly eyes, and decorate the frog's back with dark spots. Now your frog is ready to race! Just press down with your finger at the back fold to make him jump.

At the Races

To set up a racetrack for your frogs: With chalk, draw start and finish lines 3 feet apart. At the word "go," you and a friend start racing your frogs by pressing down on them. The first frog to get to the finish line wins.

 **Barking Dog**

When it comes to folding a "kid's best friend," you'll say it's easy—but the pup will simply say, "Ruff, ruff!"

• origami paper • markers • glue • scissors • pink felt

1. Begin with a square of paper in a flat diamond shape. Fold the paper in half, bringing the left corner to the right, then unfold.

2. Now fold the form in half by bringing the top point to meet the bottom.

3. Fold the left and right corners so they touch the center crease.

4. Push your finger inside the left triangle, spread it apart, and press it flat into a square. You've just done a squash fold. Repeat this step on the right side to give your puppy a pair of perky ears.

5. Fold the bottom point (front flap only) up about a third of the way for the mouth.

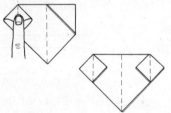

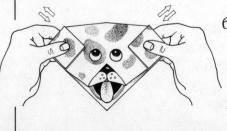

6. Use markers to draw on eyes and a nose. Cut a tongue from pink felt, and glue it inside the mouth. Give your puppy something to bark about: Hold an ear in each hand and push them toward the middle. The puppy will appear to bark!

27

One Slippery Snake

Every parent's dream of the perfect reptilian pet! This snake comes complete with its own patterned skin.

What You'll Need

• origami paper • tape • black marker • scissors • red felt or paper

Directions

1. Start out with your paper lying flat, color side down, in a diamond shape. Fold it in half, bringing the left point to the right, then unfold. Now bring the top point to the bottom and fold.

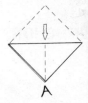

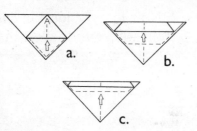

2. Bring point A (top flap only) to the top edge and fold. Bring the bottom edge of the top flap up to meet the top edge of the form and fold. Do this one more time, bringing the bottom edge of the top half up to meet the top edge of the form. Make all creases very sharp.

3. Turn the form over and repeat step 2 on the other side.

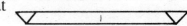

4. Unfold the entire form and lay the paper flat in a diamond shape, white side facing up. Follow the dashed lines (valley fold) and dotted lines (mountain fold) in the illustration and fold the form like an accordion. It's best to start at the bottom and work your way up.

5. Put a piece of tape on the top and bottom of the form to keep it together and make it easier to handle. At about one-third of the way in from the left point, make a diagonal crease as shown.

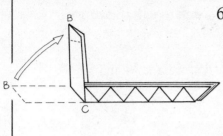

6. With one hand, hold the form by pinching point C between your fingers. With the other hand, take a finger and poke it inside the two flaps of point B. Now lift point B upward. This will turn the snake's neck inside out. Stop once the neck is vertical, and flatten the fold.

7. Make a sharp crease below point B at an angle as shown in the illustration. Open up the flaps at point B again and pull point B downward to create the head. Sharpen the folds.

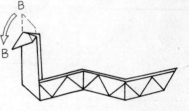

8. To help your snake stand up, make alternate vertical folds in the body in a zigzag fashion. Use a marker to draw in eyes. Cut a forked tongue from red felt or paper and tape it on.

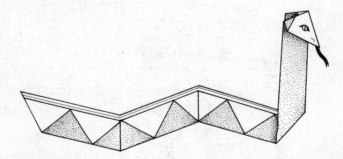

Dog or Cat House

Even paper pets need a home to call their own!

What You'll Need

• origami paper • markers

Directions

1. Begin with a square piece of paper. Fold it in half from side to side. Reopen the paper to a flat square, then fold it in half from top to bottom. Reopen the paper.

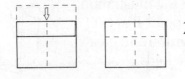

2. Fold the top edge down to the center line, then turn the form over.

3. Use a valley fold to bring the left and right sides to the center line.

4. See the little square flaps at the top? To make the roof, poke your finger into the left flap. Pull point A to the left while you squash point B to make a triangle shape. Repeat this step on the right flap.

5. Pull out sides 1 and 2 so they stand straight up from the form, and your house will stand up.

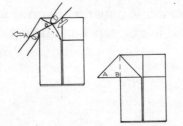

6. Use markers to draw on a doggie or kitty door, and add other details. Write the name of your pet across the roof.

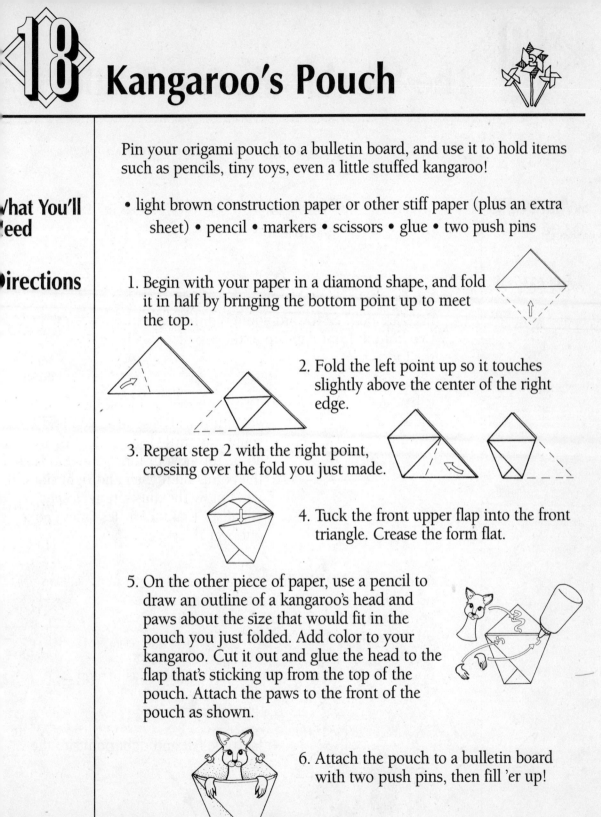

Kangaroo's Pouch

Pin your origami pouch to a bulletin board, and use it to hold items such as pencils, tiny toys, even a little stuffed kangaroo!

What You'll Need

- light brown construction paper or other stiff paper (plus an extra sheet) • pencil • markers • scissors • glue • two push pins

Directions

1. Begin with your paper in a diamond shape, and fold it in half by bringing the bottom point up to meet the top.

2. Fold the left point up so it touches slightly above the center of the right edge.

3. Repeat step 2 with the right point, crossing over the fold you just made.

4. Tuck the front upper flap into the front triangle. Crease the form flat.

5. On the other piece of paper, use a pencil to draw an outline of a kangaroo's head and paws about the size that would fit in the pouch you just folded. Add color to your kangaroo. Cut it out and glue the head to the flap that's sticking up from the top of the pouch. Attach the paws to the front of the pouch as shown.

6. Attach the pouch to a bulletin board with two push pins, then fill 'er up!

The World's Fastest Turtle

Who says turtles are slow? You can fold this one in a jiffy.

What You'll Need

• green origami paper • scissors • colored pencils
• glue • two black beads

Directions

1. Begin with Basic Form 2, and lay the form in front of you so the two loose flaps are pointed toward you. Fold the two bottom front flaps up to the top of the form.

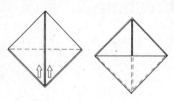

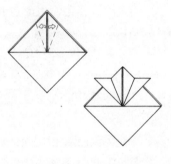

2. This form may not look like a turtle yet, but it will as soon as you fold some tiny turtle legs. To do this, start at the top of your form, and fold back the points on the left and right sides. If you follow the illustration closely, you'll see that the turtle's "toes" poke out over the edges.

3. Before you fold the other two legs, you'll need to make a cut in the form. Using your scissors, carefully snip a vertical line up the middle of the bottom half (top flap only). Stop cutting when you reach the center point. Now fold the bottom two points back as in step 2.

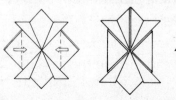

4. Fold the left and right points to the center.

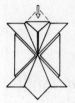

5. Now all that's left to do is let your turtle's head poke out of its shell. Start by folding the top point down so it creates a straight line along the top edge, and crease sharply.

6. Now fold the point back up, making a crease slightly below the straight top edge. Turn your form over and your turtle is complete.

7. Use colored pencils to draw a scale pattern on the shell, as well as toes on the feet. Glue on two tiny black beads for eyes.

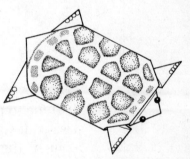

Long Live the Turtle!

Turtles appeared on Earth about 200 million years ago. Their shells give them excellent protection, which has been the secret to their successful survival. Some live on land, like this tortoise pictured here, and others live in water. Some turtles live to be 100 years old!

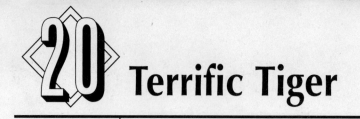

Terrific Tiger

You can give this tiger puppet a terribly scary growl.

What You'll Need

• yellow or gold origami paper
• glue • black marker • scissors • white sewing rickrack

Directions

1. Begin with Basic Form 3. Flip the form over so that the open side is facedown. Fold all four corners to the center.

2. Fold the form in half by bringing the bottom half up to meet the top half.

3. It's time to push your puppet's face into shape. Use your right thumb and index finger to "pinch" the bottom right of the form, just underneath the square flaps. Use your left hand to pinch the other side. Now push your hands toward each other as you bring the right and left upper corners to meet in the center.

4. The top two points are your tiger's ears. To round out its face, use a mountain fold to fold back the bottom left and right corners.

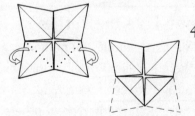

5. Open up the form, and glue the top sides to each other. Repeat this step on the bottom half. Decorate the tiger's face, and glue on white rickrack in the tiger's mouth for teeth.

A Forest for Furry Friends

Your origami friends will be happy to live among the forest of paper trees you can create!

• green origami paper

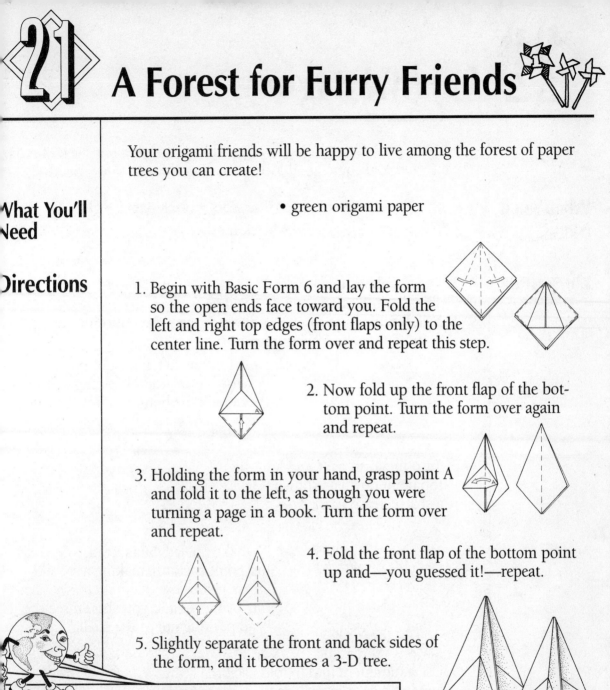

1. Begin with Basic Form 6 and lay the form so the open ends face toward you. Fold the left and right top edges (front flaps only) to the center line. Turn the form over and repeat this step.

2. Now fold up the front flap of the bottom point. Turn the form over again and repeat.

3. Holding the form in your hand, grasp point A and fold it to the left, as though you were turning a page in a book. Turn the form over and repeat.

4. Fold the front flap of the bottom point up and—you guessed it!—repeat.

5. Slightly separate the front and back sides of the form, and it becomes a 3-D tree.

Kid Power

Many animals are becoming extinct as the rain forests are torn down. Visit your local zoo. How many of the animals that you see there are endangered species? Ask your parents or teacher what you can do to help preserve the rain forests.

Lucky Ladybug

Finding a ladybug is considered good luck, so get a big stack of red paper and fold some good fortune to pass along to your friends!

What You'll Need

• red origami paper • scissors • black paper • glue
• black marker

Directions

1. Begin with a square piece of paper in a flat diamond shape, white side facing up. Fold your paper in half, bringing the top point down to meet the bottom point, and make a sharp crease.

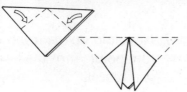

2. Now fold the left and right points down—but instead of folding them so they touch the bottom point, leave a slight gap in between.

3. Turn the form over and fold the top point down as shown. Make a sharp crease.

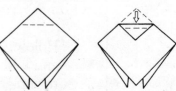

4. To make the ladybug's head, fold the top point back up, making a second crease just below the first crease. Turn the form over and you should see the head peeking out of the shell.

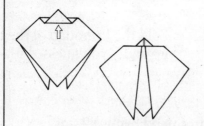

5. Use a mountain fold to fold back the right and left points, as well as the bottom point that's located underneath the ladybug's wings.

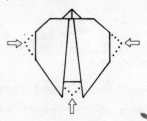

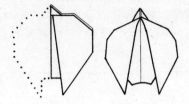

6. Fold the body in half, using a mountain fold, then open the paper until it is not quite flat. This will round out the ladybug's body.

7. Use scissors to cut out black dots, and glue them to the ladybug's back. Color in her head.

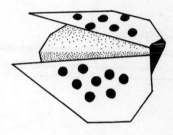

Always a Lady

It's no mystery why ladybugs—also called ladybirds—are considered lucky. They eat the insects that destroy gardens. For good luck, glue an origami ladybug to a Popsicle® stick, and prop up the stick in a potted houseplant.

Happy Crab, Crabby Crab

Everyone has mood swings, and even crabs can be happy once in a while!

What You'll Need

• red origami paper • pencil • markers

Directions

1. Start with Basic Form 1, and fold the left and right sides toward the center line.

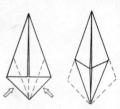

2. Turn the form on its side, then fold it in half, top meeting bottom.

3. Use a pencil to make tiny dots about a third of the way in from the right and left points as shown. Then use a valley fold to fold the points so they face downward, bending them at the spots you just marked. Crease them well.

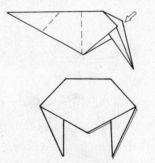

4. The points facing down will be the crab's legs. Take the crab's right leg and unfold it. Lift the bottom right point out as shown, then poke the leg between the two sides of the form with a squash fold. Repeat this step on the left leg.

5. Draw a happy face on one side of your crab. Flip him over and draw a crabby face on the other side.

Swan Lake

Transform plain white paper into a graceful swan that looks beautiful atop any special birthday or wedding gift.

• white origami paper • orange and black markers

What You'll Need

Directions

1. Begin with Basic Form 1, and lay the form so that the narrow point faces right. Fold the lower side so it meets the center line. Repeat this step with the upper side.

2. Use a valley fold to fold the form in half, bringing the top half to meet the bottom half.

3. Your swan needs a long, graceful neck. Pull point A upward, making a crease as shown. Unfold it. Pull up on point A while you push down on the two creases with your fingers. This will angle the neck upward. (The neck will turn inside out!)

4. For the swan's head, bring point A down at an angle and crease, then unfold it. Now push point B to the left while you pull point A down, allowing the form to bend at the crease. Once the head is in place, crease it flat.

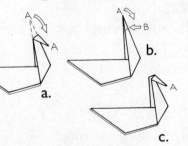

5. Use markers to color the beak orange, and create a black mask around the eyes. Spread out the base so the swan can sit on its own.

Goin' Batty

Hide your origami bats in backyard trees or in hanging houseplants, and they may be mistaken for real vampire bats!

What You'll Need

• black origami paper • glue • scissors • black felt-tip marker • paintbrush • puff paints (glow-in-the-dark optional)

Directions

1. Begin with a sheet of paper in a diamond shape, then fold it in half by bringing the bottom point up to the top. Now fold the bottom edge two-thirds of the way up.

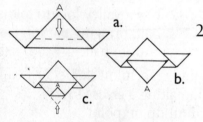

2. Turn the form over, and fold down point A (just the front flap) partway. Fold the tip of A back up again. You've just made the body and wings of your bat.

3. Fold the form in half, in a valley fold, left to right. Use a valley fold as shown to bring the front flap, which is on the right, to the left. Then use a mountain fold to fold the back flap. The bat's wings should be lying flat against each other.

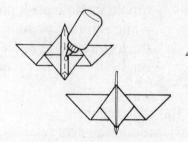

4. Now open up the wings so that they are perpendicular to the bat's body. Glue the area at the back of the bat's body where the wings meet.

5. To make the bat's head, hold the tip of point B and push it down flat until it forms a square. Dab some glue inside the head so it will lie closer to the body.

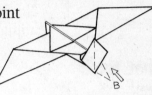

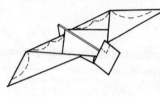

6. Using scissors, cut away the areas shown by the dotted lines in the illustration. This will form your bat's ears and give a wavy edge to its wings.

7. Color any exposed white areas with a black felt-tip marker. Use dots of puff paint to create yellow eyes and a red mouth.

Keeping Their Eyes and Ears Open

Bats use their ears as well as their eyes to see. When a bat knows that a tasty insect is nearby, it tries to find it by sending out sound waves that are reflected off the insect back to the bat. This is called echolocation. That's why bats often fly back and forth in odd ways.

A Barn for Your Brood

This barn makes the perfect backdrop for the menagerie of farm animals you can make in this book!

What You'll Need

• origami paper, 20 inches square

Directions

1. Begin with Basic Form 5. Fold point A and point C up (front flaps only) to meet point B. Turn the form over and repeat this step with the remaining layer.

2. You now have a diamond shape. Fold this in half, bottom meeting top, and unfold. Open up the triangle on the right side and bring point D to meet point E, forming a square.

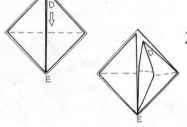

3. Lift up the triangle on the left side and bring point F to point E to form a square. Turn the form over and repeat step 2 and this step on the other side.

4. Fold the right and left outside edges to the center to make a crease (top flaps only), then unfold them.

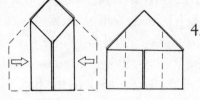

5. Fold and unfold small triangle shapes on the inside corner of each door to make creases as shown.

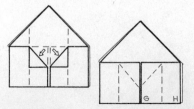

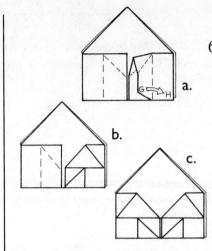

6. Ready to make the large front door? First, bring point G to meet point H (top flap only). As you do this, push your thumb inside the triangle that's formed by the crease you made in step 5. Squash it flat into a triangle using your index finger. If it looks like you just folded a mini-house, you're almost there! Just repeat this step on the left side.

a.

b.

c.

7. To finish, fold the center triangle up. Using a marking pen or pencil, draw a hayloft window above the doors.

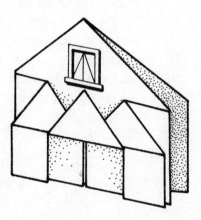

Crazy Critter Mask

Is it a bird? Is it a plane? When you make this crazy mask, it can be almost any animal in the world—or even one that's out of this world!

What You'll Need

• stiff paper, such as construction paper, cut about 12 inches square • scissors • string • glue • feathers, buttons, markers, or other decorations

Directions

1. Begin with Basic Form 1, and fold the top point down so your form now has a straight, horizontal top edge.

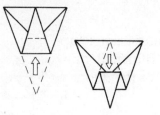

2. Fold the bottom point up so it touches the center of the top edge, then fold the point down so it sticks below the bottom. This will be your crazy critter's nose.

3. Use a mountain fold to fold the form in half lengthwise. Hold it in one hand while you pull the nose up and to the right. Crease sharply at the back of the nose so that it stays firmly in place.

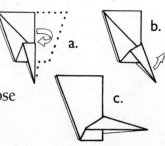

4. You may need an adult's help with this next step. Reopen the mask and cut out holes for eyes, then use the points of your scissors to pierce a hole on each side of the mask near the eyes. Knot a string through each hole so the mask can be placed around your head.

5. All that's left to do is decorate your mask using feathers, buttons, markers, or anything you like—then wear it proudly or hang it on your wall.

Crazy Critter Show

Attaching a mask to a stick to make a puppet is a tradition as old as masks themselves! Why not create a cast of crazy critter masks, then put on a puppet show? To make your puppets, skip step 4 in which you attach a string. Instead, tape each mask to the top of a yardstick, placing it down far enough so it doesn't flop around. When it's show time, move your puppet around by holding the bottom of the stick to make your character "talk."

28 One-Ton Elephant

Making this jungle giant from a tiny piece of paper is a ton of fun!

What You'll Need

• gray origami paper • scissors • marker

Directions

1. Start with Basic Form 1, and lay it flat on your table with the narrow point facing up and left, like you see in the illustration here. Then fold it in half by bringing the top right edge over to the bottom left.

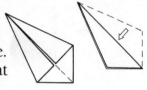

2. Fold point A over so it faces right (as you do this, you'll make a diagonal crease about two-thirds of the way down your form).

3. Make another fold by bringing point A to the left at the dotted line and creasing sharply.

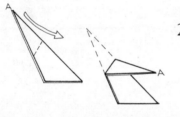

4. Ready to make your elephant's head? Carefully lift point A and poke your fingers inside the flaps. Then squash it flat, creasing all the folds sharply.

5. Pull out point B on each side of the head to make the ears stick out.

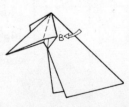

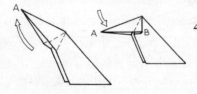

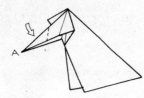

6. See the trunk? Crease and uncrease the trunk at the dotted line as shown. Now separate the two flaps and bring point A down between them using a squash fold.

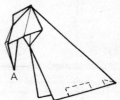

7. Use scissors to cut out the legs and tail as you see in the illustration. With the marker, draw in eyes, tusks, and toenails.

A Really Big Bite

Did you know that an adult elephant eats up to 440 pounds of food a day? In fact, it chews so much grass, leaves, twigs, and fruit that a normal elephant wears out six sets of teeth in its lifetime! Now, aren't you glad your elephant is made only of paper?

Gentle Giraffe

This gentle giraffe is a two-part form. When you put it together, watch its long neck grow!

What You'll Need

- yellow origami paper, 8 inches and 4 inches square, one sheet each
  - scissors • glue or tape • brown marker • embroidery thread

Directions

1. Make the giraffe's body by folding a crab (see page 38) using the 8-inch piece of yellow paper, only don't decorate it. Set it aside.

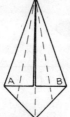

2. For the neck, begin with the 4-inch piece of paper and fold Basic Form 1.

3. Fold points A and B to the center as shown.

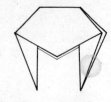

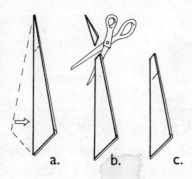

4. Bring the left to the right side using a valley fold to fold the form in half. Do you have your scissors handy? Carefully cut a diagonal line an inch from the top of your form. Now make another partial cut ¾ inch down from the first.

5. Slightly reopen the form, and with your finger on the top right edge, push down on the tip to make the giraffe's head. Gently reclose the form. The head should now be tucked neatly between the two sides of the neck and its ears!

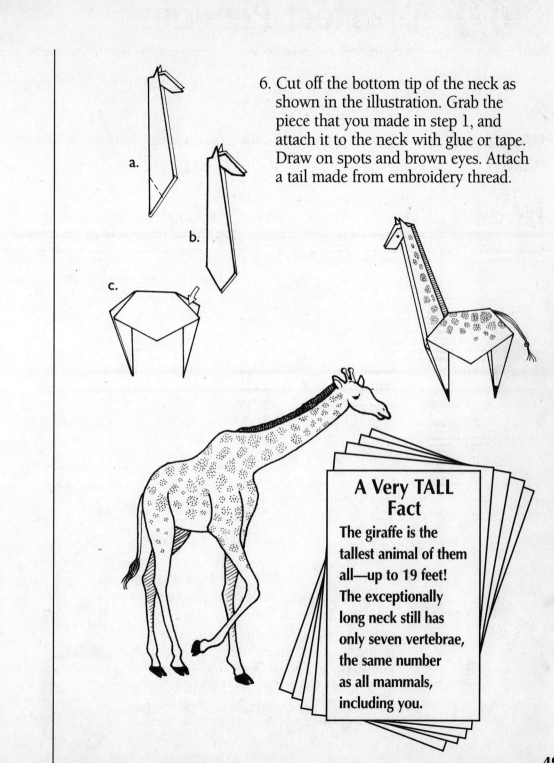

6. Cut off the bottom tip of the neck as shown in the illustration. Grab the piece that you made in step 1, and attach it to the neck with glue or tape. Draw on spots and brown eyes. Attach a tail made from embroidery thread.

a.

b.

c.

A Very TALL Fact

The giraffe is the tallest animal of them all—up to 19 feet! The exceptionally long neck still has only seven vertebrae, the same number as all mammals, including you.

A Perfect Penguin

Use paper that's black on one side and white on the other to give your penguin his proper tuxedo attire.

What You'll Need

- origami paper (black on one side, white on the other)
- glue • two googly eyes

Directions

1. Start with your paper in a diamond shape, black side facing up. Fold the bottom point up about a third of the way.

2. Now fold the form in half by bringing the right side over to the left.

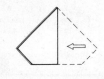

3. Use a valley fold to fold the left point (front flap only) until it just touches the right side—this will be the penguin's flipper. Now turn the form over and repeat this step on the other side.

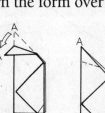

4. Fold down point A about 1½ inches from the tip as shown. Make a sharp crease and unfold it.

5. To create a head, first slightly reopen the form. Pull down on point A, allowing the form to bend along the crease you created in step 4. Continue pushing point A toward the center until the form automatically closes back up. Lay the form down, and flatten all folds. Glue on two googly eyes, and admire your perfect penguin in his "tux and tails"!

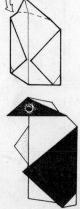

 31 Flapping Bird

The flapping bird is a traditional origami form that gets its name from—you guessed it!—the fact that its wings can flap.

• origami paper • black marker

What You'll Need

Directions

1. Begin with Basic Form 7, and lay it vertically so the points that separate are facing toward you. Crease each side by folding on the dotted lines as shown in the illustration, then unfolding.

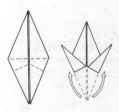

2. Gently separate the two flaps at the bottom of the form. Lift the lower left point so it sticks upward, bending it at the crease you made in step 1. Tuck it inside the form, using a squash fold. Repeat this step on the right side.

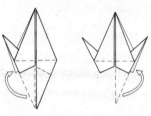

3. To make the head, fold down point A at an angle as shown, then unfold it. Push point A down with a squash fold to complete the head.

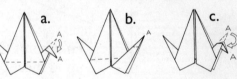
a.   b.   c.

4. Fold the top point down at an angle (front flap only) to form a wing as shown. Repeat on the other side. Use a black marker to draw in eyes.

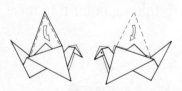

5. Lift the wings to be perpendicular to the body. With one hand, grasp the bird at the pointed base just below the head. Grasp the tail with the other hand. Pull the tail to the back and watch your bird flap its wings!

Snapping Alligator

It's a lucky thing that you control the jaws of this alligator puppet—otherwise he might just take a bite out of you!

What You'll Need

• green origami paper • markers • glue • white sewing rickrack

Directions

1. Begin with the first step in Basic Form 4. Lay the form down horizontally, and bring the left half to the right with a valley fold.

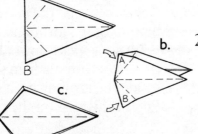

2. Bring points A and B to the center line and fold sharply. Now unfold them. Squash-fold points A and B to the inside of the form and crease flat.

3. Fold point C (front flap only) up to meet point D.

4. Turn the form over and repeat step 3, folding point E to meet point D.

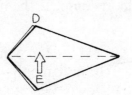

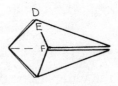

5. Fold back point F, then turn the form over and repeat this step on the other side to create small flaps.

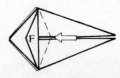

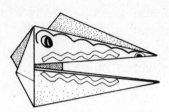

6. Draw on eyes and a bumpy snout. Add sharp teeth by gluing on strips of white sewing rickrack along your gator's long jaws.

7. To make the alligator snap, grasp the small flaps at the sides and pull your hands apart.

Alligator or Crocodile?

A big pair of jaws is about to chomp down on you! But wait—how do you know if it's a crocodile or an alligator? The trick is to look at its closed jaws. A crocodile's fourth lower tooth will stick up outside the mouth, whereas all of an alligator's teeth are hidden inside the mouth.

A Family of Butterflies

This cute butterfly mobile shows that a family who flies together stays together!

• origami paper, at least 4 sheets • pipe cleaners • glue • cut paper or rhinestones • scissors • white thread • needle • branch

Directions

1. Begin with Basic Form 8 and use a mountain fold to fold the form in half, open side up.

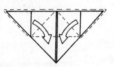

2. Fold the left and right corners down as shown.

3. Turn the form over, then fold it in half and unfold it to make a sharp crease between the butterfly's wings. Turn out points A and B to give the back of each wing more shape.

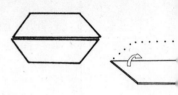

4. Repeat steps 1 through 3 to create your family of butterflies. You'll want to make at least three or four little creatures.

5. With pipe cleaners, add antennae and a body to each butterfly. Put a line of glue along the center fold of the butterfly. Take a 12-inch pipe cleaner and fold it in half. Slip it onto the butterfly, half of the pipe cleaner going on top of the glue and the other half going on the underside as shown.

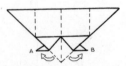

6. Twist the pipe cleaner together to form the head. Gently bend the pipe cleaner ends out to look like antennae. Decorate your butterflies with cut paper or rhinestones.

7. Now you are ready to make your mobile. First, cut off a 20- to 30-inch length of thread and thread it into a needle. Push the needle down through the top of one wing, then back up through the other wing. Tie a knot, leaving the longer thread for hanging. Do this for each butterfly.

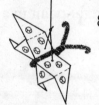

8. Complete your mobile by tying the other end of each thread to your branch. Hang your branch from an additional piece of thread in an open doorway or from the ceiling.

Now You See It, Now You Don't

You don't need a net to capture some beautiful, realistic butterflies! Just fold up origami butterflies, then fashion them after real ones, such as the Admiral butterfly. Its wings are orange, yellow, and black. Its underside, which is brown, provides instant camouflage for the butterfly when its wings are closed.

Circus Seal

With a ball delicately balanced on its nose, this seal is ready to make its way to the big top—and straight into your heart!

What You'll Need

• origami paper • scissors • markers • colored paper • glue

Directions

1. Start with Basic Form 1, and lay it flat on your surface with the narrow point facing left. Turn the form over. Fold the right point in a valley fold as shown.

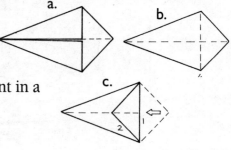

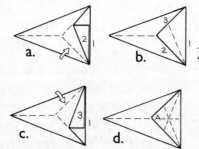

2. Fold side 2 to meet side 1 as shown and crease it sharply, then unfold. Repeat this step with side 3 meeting side 1, then unfold.

3. If you've made all your creases carefully, this next step will be easy. Pinch point A in a valley fold, pulling it to the right and allowing the form to bend at the creases you made in step 2. Continue moving point A until it becomes a "peak" perpendicular to the form. The rest of the form should now be flat.

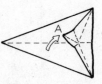

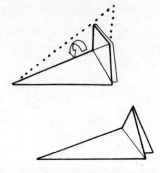

4. Now use a mountain fold to fold your form in half. Remember the little "peak"? It is now the seal's head.

5. Every seal needs flippers to clap with, which you can make by folding points B and C back.

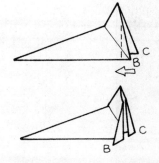

6. Make a vertical crease near the seal's tail by folding and unfolding the left point. Then use scissors to make a small cut along the center fold of the seal's backbone, stopping at the crease. Separate the pieces to make the tail.

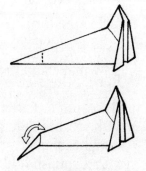

7. Draw in eyes and a nose. To make a ball, cut a circle out of colored paper, and decorate it using colorful markers. Glue it to the tip of your seal's nose, and it is sure to earn the origami "seal" of approval!

Nest, Sweet Nest

Here's a bird that never needs to find a place for her eggs—her nest is built right in!

What You'll Need

- origami paper, at least 7 inches square
- black marker • straw or plastic grass • plastic egg

Directions

1. Begin with Basic Form 1, and lay it flat so the narrow point is facing left. Use a mountain fold to fold it in half, bringing the bottom back to meet the top.

2. Make a crease by folding point A up as shown in the illustration, then unfolding it.

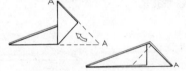

3. Carefully open the right side of the form so you can lift point A up and tuck it inside the form with a squash fold.

4. Now make another crease by folding point B up diagonally and unfolding it. Partially open the left side of the form while you lift point B straight up and tuck it inside the form with a squash fold.

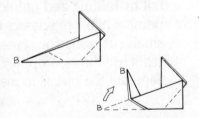

5. Make one more crease just below point B. Then poke the tip down in a squash fold to form a beak.

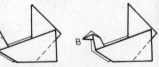

6. Fold points C and D straight out from the form using the existing creases. Now when you set your birdie down, it will stay steady.

7. Using a black marker, draw in the eyes. The middle of the bird's body forms a cozy nest where you can put the straw and egg.

58

36 A Whale of a Goat

Just three steps and you have a whale that's afloat. One more fold, and it turns into a goat!

What You'll Need

• gray origami paper • markers • scissors • glue • yarn

Directions

1. Begin with Basic Form 1, making sharp creases. Unfold. Starting at the opposite end, fold Basic Form 1 again, this time leaving it folded. Lay it so the wide end points to your right.

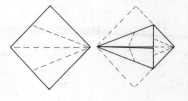

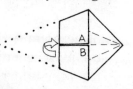

2. Fold the left side back to meet the right using a mountain fold.

3. With your forefinger, reach under point A and bring it over to the left as far as it will go. At the same time, push side 1 down to the center. Crease the form flat. Repeat this step with point B and side 2 and your whale is complete.

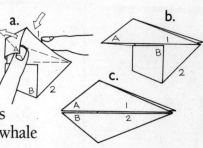

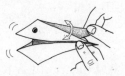

4. Draw on eyes, then hold each side of the tail and move your hands apart to make the whale's mouth move.

5. To change your whale into a goat, just fold down one side of the whale's tail to form a floppy ear. Turn the form over and repeat this step. Glue on a few short lengths of yarn to create the billygoat's beard.

Handsome Hamster

You'll never need to clean a cage or worry about daily feedings when you keep a paper hamster as a pet!

What You'll Need

• origami paper (plus an extra sheet) • scissors • glue • black marker

Directions

1. Start with Basic Form 8, then use a mountain fold to fold it in half, bringing the bottom edge up to meet the top edge.

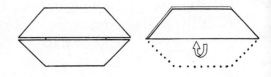

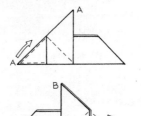

2. Bring point A (front flap only) straight up, making a diagonal crease that runs from the upper left point to the bottom center of the form. Turn the form over and repeat this step with point B on the other side.

3. Now grasp side 1 and fold it down along the crease as you see in the illustration. (Notice the movement of point B.) Turn the form over and repeat this step on the other side.

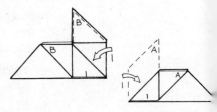

4. Fold point A to the left as though it were a page in a book. This will give your hamster an ear. Now turn your form over and repeat this step to make the other ear.

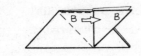

5. Create feet by folding the two back bottom points forward and out. To round off the nose and ears, squash-fold in the tips of points C, D, and E.

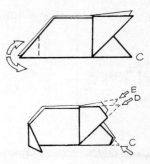

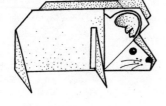

6. Add two front legs by cutting out two triangle shapes from scrap paper and securing them in place with glue. With a black marker, draw in facial features.

A Secret Hamster Hiding Place

Hamsters store food in a hidden place: their cheeks. It's not as secret as they think, however, because often their cheeks can puff up so big, it looks like they swallowed a tennis ball! You can use your hamster to pass a hidden message. Begin with your flat sheet of origami paper in front of you, and write a message on the white side. Then fold the hamster following the instructions. Only someone who unfolds the origami will see your secret message!

Friendly Gorilla

You'll go "ape" over this happy-go-lucky gorilla.

What You'll Need

• black origami paper • white pencil (grease pencil works best)

Directions

1. Begin with Basic Form 3, then turn your form over.

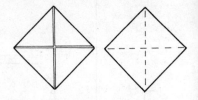

2. Fold each of the corners to the center.

3. Turn the form over again. Just like you did in step 2, fold each of the corners to the center. As your form gets smaller, it will become harder to fold.

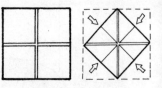

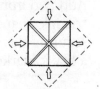

4. Turn your form over once more, and lay it flat in a diamond shape. Just above the bottom point are two triangles that form a square. Separate the two triangles at the center opening while you push down on point A. Now it's a rectangle and the base of your gorilla.

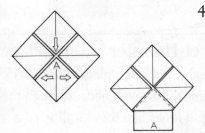

5. Turn the form over. Unfold the four triangles (top flaps only). Turn the form over again. Pull points B and C outward and unfold. Again, turn the form over.

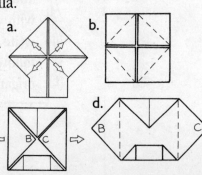

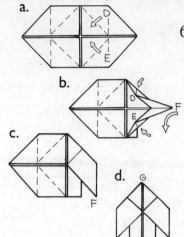

a.

b.

c.

d.

6. Like any other ape, your furry friend's arms hang low to the ground. To make the right arm, pinch points D and E toward the center until they meet in the middle. Pull point F downward and flatten the form. Repeat this step to make the left arm.

7. To make the head, push down on point G. The head will automatically pop up.

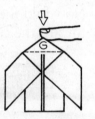

8. Your gorilla is almost ready! Fold the form in half using a valley fold, bringing the arms together in front. Your gorilla will now be able to stand up on its own by resting on the base and both arms. Use a white pencil to draw in a friendly face.

Here, Piggy, Piggy!

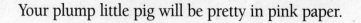

Your plump little pig will be pretty in pink paper.

What You'll Need

• pink origami paper • scissors • pink curling ribbon
• glue • black marker

Directions

1. Begin with a square piece of paper. Crease your paper by folding it in half from top to bottom, then unfolding it. Now fold the top and bottom edges toward the center line.

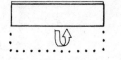

2. Use a mountain fold to fold the form in half, bringing the bottom up to the top.

3. Bring the right and left sides to meet in the center, fold the form flat, and then unfold. Bring points A and B (top flap only) to the bottom edge and then unfold.

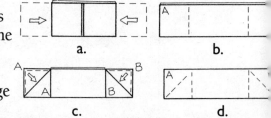

a.

b.

c.

d.

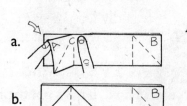

a.

b.

c.

4. Place your right index finger just to the right of point C. With the index finger of your left hand, open up the front flap of point A, and pull point A down to the bottom edge of the form. Crease the form flat. Repeat this step for point B.

5. Turn the form over and repeat steps 3 and 4 on the other side.

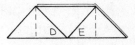

6. Fold points D and E so they point straight down below the bottom edge of the form. Turn your form over and repeat on the other side for points F and G.

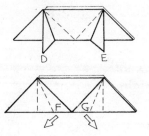

7. See the left point? Make it into a snout by "sinking" it into the pig's body using a squash fold. Round off the pig's back end with a bigger squash fold than you did for the snout. Glue on a length of curled ribbon for a corkscrew tail. Draw in eyes and a mouth, using a black marker.

Happy As a Pig in Mud

Pigs love to roll around in mud, but it's not because they're dirty creatures. Pigs don't sweat, so the mud helps cool their bodies on a hot day. Create a realistic pig pen for your paper pal by shoveling dirt into an overturned shoe box lid. Use a small cardboard box, like one that holds jewelry or a watch, as a feeding trough.

The puffer fish may look sweet, but with a little air—watch out! It quickly expands to twice its size.

What You'll Need

- origami paper (plus an extra sheet) • markers • scissors • glue • two googly eyes

Directions

1. Begin with Basic Form 5 and fold the lower left and right corners (front flaps only) to the top point; then turn the form over and repeat this step.

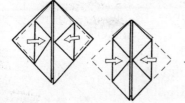

2. Now fold the front flaps so the right and left points touch the center line. Turn the form over again and repeat this step on the other side.

3. Fold and unfold points A and B (front flaps only), making sharp creases, then unfold.

4. Next, tuck points A and B into the center triangles as shown in the illustration. To do this, open the triangle pockets with your fingers and slip the edges in. This step takes practice, so don't be frustrated if you can't quite get it to fit at first.

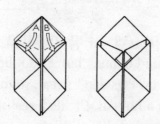

5. Turn your form over and repeat steps 3 and 4 on the other side. Pick up the right (top) flap and bring it to the left, as though you were turning a page of a book. The plain side of the form should now be showing. Turn the form over and repeat.

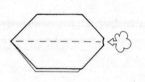

6. Find the tiny hole at the bottom of your form. When you blow into it, your fish will inflate right before your eyes.

7. Decorate your puffy pal with markers, and cut a tail fin and four smaller fins out of the extra paper. Glue them onto your puffed-up puffer, along with a pair of googly eyes.

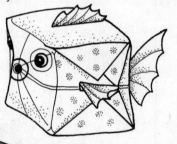

What a Surprise!

Nature has a way of protecting its creatures. If the puffer fish is pulled from the water, it fills with air to look big, scary, and inedible. Often, the unsuspecting animal (or human!) who catches it quickly tosses back the fish, which slowly returns to its normal size. Your origami puffer fish, however, is definitely a keeper!

Dinnertime!

Decorate this cute dish to look just like your dog or cat, and watch it eat all the way to the bottom to see its "reflection."

• sturdy paper, at least 14 inches square
• tape • scissors • paper •glue • permanent markers

1. Begin with Basic Form 6. With the open end facing up, fold the upper edges on the right and left sides (front flaps only) to the center.

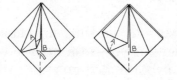

2. Open up the left triangle and move point A toward the left edge, then flatten as shown. Repeat this step with point B.

3. Turn the form over, and repeat steps 1 and 2 on the other side.

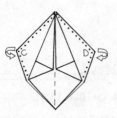

4. Now you are ready to grasp point C (front flap only) and use a mountain fold to fold it back into the center between the front and back flaps. Repeat with point D, then turn the form over and repeat on the opposite side.

5. Using valley folds, fold and unfold the top point (all flaps) down and the bottom point (all flaps) up, creating creases as shown by the dotted lines in the illustration.

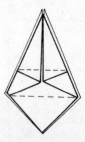

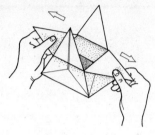

6. At the top of your form are four open points. To make your dish take shape, grasp the two outer points and pull outward. Now flatten the base into a box shape.

7. Tape two of the points to the bottom outside of the bowl. The other two triangles are the ears. Cut a square piece of paper slightly smaller than the bottom of the bowl. With permanent markers, draw your pet's face. Glue your drawing to the bottom inside of the bowl. Draw details on the two ears and write your pet's name on the outside of the bowl. If it's okay with your parents, this bowl can be used to hold dry puppy food or kitty food.

Mirror, Mirror, on My Dish . . .

Want to make your pet's reflection more realistic? Take a photo of your pet and use scissors to cut it to a shape that fits the dish. Glue it in place, then watch to see if your pet recognizes that gorgeous creature at the bottom!

A Horse, of Course

Fold 'em, cowboy! Even city slickers will enjoy making this paper pony.

What You'll Need

• origami paper • scissors • yarn • glue • markers

Directions

1. Begin with Basic Form 1, and lay it so the narrow point is facing away from you. Then fold the bottom point up, tucking it under the two flaps.

2. Fold point A so the front flap points left. Repeat this step with point B, then turn your form over.

3. Now fold points C and D so they meet at the center of your form. Turn the form over.

4. Fold point E down and to the left toward point F. Make a sharp crease, then unfold. Now bring point E down and to the right toward point G. Fold sharply and then unfold.

5. Fold the top point over toward the bottom in a mountain fold. The point will extend beyond the bottom of the form. Now unfold it.

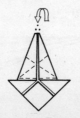

6. Fold the top point down using a mountain fold.

7. Do you see the diamond shape in the lower section of your form? Using your thumb and forefinger, grasp the top point of the diamond, then pull it downward. At the same time, fold the form in half in a valley fold by bringing the left side to the right side. The horse's neck will automatically pop up as it bends along all those creases you previously made. Fold form flat.

8. Your horse is really starting to take shape! To make the head, fold the top point down at an angle as shown, then unfold it. Pull the tip down and tuck it inside the form using a squash fold to complete the head.

9. Make a tail and mane from yarn, and glue them onto your horse. Draw in eyes, nostrils, and hooves. You can even draw in a saddle!

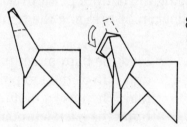

A Horse of a Different Stripe

Want to make a zebra? Start by folding the horse using white paper. Zebras have rounded ears, which you can make by cutting small circles from paper, then gluing them to the head of your form. Use a black marker to add vertical and horizontal stripes. Don't worry about getting them exactly right. Like a human's fingerprints, no two zebras' stripes are alike.

43 Crazy Like a Fox

From pointy ears to bushy tail, you'd be crazy not to love this fox.

What You'll Need

• origami paper • marker

Directions

1. Start with your paper in a diamond shape, then fold it in half by bringing the bottom point over to the top. Fold it in half again by bringing the right point to meet the left.

2. Fold the bottom left point (front flap only) up to the top point using a valley fold. Then use a mountain fold to bring the back left point to the top. Rotate your form a quarter turn counterclockwise, as shown in the illustration, so the open ends are to the bottom and left.

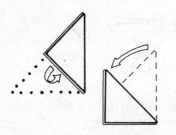

(open ends)

3. Fold the left edge over toward the right and crease sharply on the dotted line. Then lift the top three flaps so they stick up straight from the rest of the form.

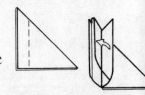

4. Separate the two left flaps from the one right flap, and flatten the form. At the same time, you'll need to push the tip of the middle flap downward while you squash it flat. You've just made the fox's head.

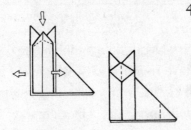

5. To make the tail, simply fold the bottom right point to the left. Use a marker to draw in a "foxy" face and other details.

72

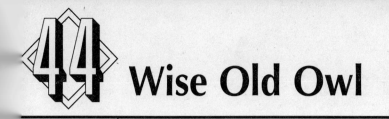

Wise Old Owl

Whoooooooooo's afraid of an owl? Not you!

- origami paper (plus an extra sheet) • scissors • tape
- black and yellow markers

Directions

1. Begin with Basic Form 7, and lay it flat on a surface with the points that can separate facing toward you. Fold the form in half by bringing the front flap of the top point down to the bottom. Turn the form over and repeat this step on the other side.

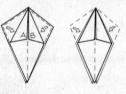

2. Fold points A and B (front flap only) toward the center crease. Turn the form over and repeat this step on the other side.

3. Wondering where the wings are? They're tucked inside the form. To bring a wing up, reach inside the form on one side and pull the inner flaps from the bottom upward. As you do this, slightly twist the wing forward. Once the wing is out, flatten the form. Repeat this step on the other wing.

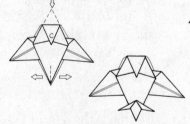

4. To make the head, fold down point C as shown in a valley fold. Use scissors to carefully cut a vertical line at the bottom point (front flap only) as shown. Fold one piece to the left and the other to the right for the tail.

5. Cut out two small triangles for ears. Tape them onto the owl. Use a black marker to draw in eyes and other details. Color the beak and a thin circle around the eyes yellow.

Paper Panda

Here's one panda that will never be declared an endangered species as long as there's plenty of paper around.

What You'll Need

- black origami paper (white on the other side)
- white crayon or pencil (grease pencil works well)

Directions

1. Begin with your paper in a square, white side up. Fold it in half vertically, crease, and unfold. Then fold the top left and right points down to the center crease. Turn your form over.

2. Fold the left and right sides toward the center.

3. Reach to the back of the form and pull out the left and right points. You should now have a diamond shape at the top of your form. Fold point A down to the bottom point of the diamond shape.

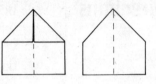

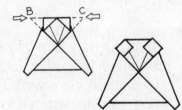

4. To make your panda's ears, fold points B and C toward the center. Poke your finger into the left ear, lift it out, then squash it flat. Repeat this step on the right ear.

5. Use a mountain fold to bring back the top of the panda's head so that the fold is at the center of the ears. The front flap of each ear will rise naturally. Flatten them out. Form the nose by folding up the bottom tip of the triangle (front flap only).

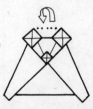

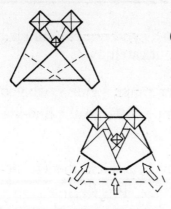

6. Look closely at the illustration for this next step. Fold the lower right corner up so the black tip tucks just slightly under the pocket above the nose. Repeat this step on the other side, and you're nearly finished!

7. Use a mountain fold to fold back the point of the chin. Use a white crayon or pencil to draw in the eyes.

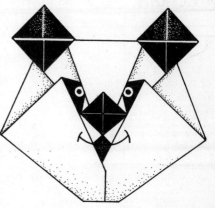

Protecting the Panda

China's giant panda is probably the most famous endangered animal. Only about a thousand still exist in the world. Ask a parent or teacher to help you write a letter to your congressional leaders letting them know that you care about pandas. If you really want your letter to get noticed, try writing it on the back of an origami panda!

46 Fluffy Bunny

At Eastertime (or anytime!) you can put mini jelly beans into this bunny's mouth if you do it carefully.

What You'll Need

• origami paper • tape • glue • two googly eyes
• pink pompom • cotton ball • fine-line marker

Directions

1. Begin with Basic Form 5, and fold the left and right corners (front flaps only) up to the tip.

2. Your form should now look like a diamond on top of a triangle. Fold the right and left corners of the diamond so they touch the center line.

3. Fold and unfold points A and B (front flaps only) to make a sharp crease. Next, tuck points A and B into the center triangles as shown. To do this, open the triangle pockets and slip the edges in.

4. Flip your form over. Use a valley fold to bring the left side to the center line (the lower left corner should now be pointing down). Repeat this step on the right side.

5. Ready to make your bunny's big ears? Grasp the lower left point and fold it back along the dotted line as shown. Repeat with the lower right point.

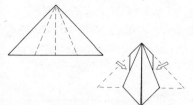

6. Fold point C so it touches the center. Repeat with point D. Tape down the ears to the form.

7. Find the tiny hole at the end of your form. Blow into it, and your bunny will come to life! Glue on two googly eyes, a pink pompom nose, and a cotton ball tail. Draw in whiskers, using a fine-line marker.

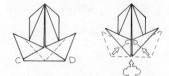

Fabulous Flamingo

Using white paper, you can make a traditional Japanese good-luck crane. With bright pink paper, it turns into a feathery flamingo.

• white or bright pink origami paper • black marker

1. Begin with Basic Form 7, and lay it flat on a surface. The end that has an opening between the two sides should point down.

2. Fold the left and right points (top layer only) toward the center line so the bottom edges lie flat against the center line. Turn your form over and repeat this step on the other side.

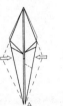

3. Your flamingo's neck can be formed by making a diagonal crease on the bottom right flap of the form, as shown in the illustration, then unfolding. Lift point A up again, separating the two sides of the piece. This part of the form will now turn inside out.

4. Grasp the neck about one-third of the way down from the tip. Gently pull point A down. While you do this, the neck will automatically open up and will tuck inside the head. Stop moving point A once the head is in position, and flatten all folds.

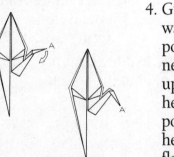

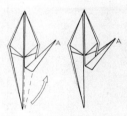

5. The top two points are the wings. Pull them out and away from each other until the flamingo's body fills out. Use a black marker to make small dots for eyes.

Snorting Bull

Once you make this bull, you'd better keep all your red paper out of sight or he's likely to charge!

**What You'll
Need**

• origami paper, at least 8 inches square • scissors • tape • markers

Directions

1. Begin with Basic Form 7, with the two separated flaps at the bottom. Fold the top point (front flap only) to the bottom. Turn the form over.

2. Use scissors to carefully make a straight cut from the top point down to the middle of the form.

3. To make the bull's horns, fold point A so it points left and point B so it points right. Now fold point A and B back up as shown.

4. To make the ears, fold points C and D up and outward. Crease sharply. Fold down the top point of the head. Place a piece of tape in the center of where all the folds meet to help the form stay flat. Turn the form over.

5. To make the snout, fold the bottom point up as shown. Fold the bottom up one more time.

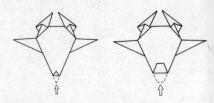

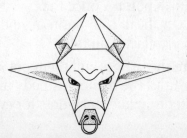

6. Draw in eyes and other details. If you want, add a thin wire nose ring as shown in the illustration. Toro! Toro!

Tom Turkey

Create a turkey so true-to-life that people may be tempted to "gobble" it right up.

What You'll Need

• brown origami paper • glue • craft feathers • scissors
• red felt • black marker

Directions

1. Begin with Basic Form 1, and fold the left and right sides toward the center line.

2. Use a mountain fold to fold back the top point. Now use a mountain fold to fold the form in half by bringing the left side to the right. Crease sharply, then unfold.

3. Bring point A up until it extends beyond the top edge of the form and fold. Pull point A back up, and at the same time, pinch the right and left sides of the piece you are lifting. Stop pulling point A once the form resembles a spatula.

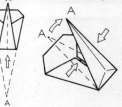

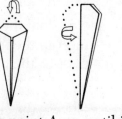

4. Fold points B and C out past the side edges. Bend the tail portion up as shown and make a crease. This creates a base so your turkey can stand on its own.

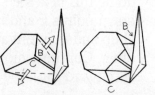

5. Bend the tip of point A forward and down for the beak. No turkey is complete without a little dressing! Decorate your turkey by gluing on craft feathers and a small wattle from red felt. Draw in eyes and other details with a black marker.

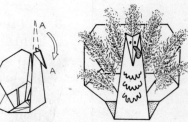

Fold a floating ship that will hold all your origami animals . . . two by two by two. What a great way to display your talents!

What You'll Need

• construction paper, at least 14 inches square • tape • markers

Directions

1. Begin with the first step of Basic Form 3. Fold the right and left sides to meet in the middle.

2. Now fold the bottom and top edges to meet in the middle and make sharp creases, then unfold.

3. Make two diagonal creases across the center four squares only. To do this, fold point A to meet point B, then unfold. Repeat this step on the opposite side, bringing point C to meet point D, then unfold.

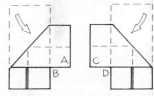

4. Look at the illustration carefully when doing this next step. While holding down points E and F, lift points G and H up and then out away from each other. Continue moving points G and H outward until the form flattens.

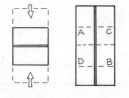

5. Pull the top edge down to meet the center of the form and crease sharply. A few pieces of tape will help secure the bottom layer to lie flat. Leave the top layer free so you can store your origami menagerie inside. Use markers to draw in details.

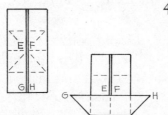